# JOURNEYING TOWARD WISDOM

## Anthony Carrozzo OFM

### Artwork by

## Michael Reyes OFM

FRANCISCAN
PUBLISHING

Journeying Toward Wisdom
First Edition 2023

Copyright © The Franciscan Publishing Company Ltd 2023.
www.franciscanpublishing.com

Published by The Franciscan Publishing Company Ltd, Darlington,
Co. Durham, United Kingdom.

The moral rights of the author, Anthony Carrozzo OFM,
have been asserted.

ISBN 978-1-9151981-1-2


The front cover image is from a painting by Michael Reyes OFM.
Used with permission and gratitude.

Paintings of the Vows/Virtues within the text are also by Michael
Reyes OFM, and are owned by the Vocation Ministry of Holy
Name Province, New York City. Printed with the permission of
Basil Valente OFM, Vocation Director.


Cover design by Sadie Butterworth-Jones


Printed by Newton Press, Blue Bridge Centre,
St. Cuthbert's Way, Newton Aycliffe DL5 6DS
on sustainably sourced paper and card,
using vegetable based inks on a waterless
printing press.

FSC

In gratitude to

Holy Name Province,

always my home.

# Contents

# JOURNEYING TOWARD WISDOM

## Introduction

There was a time when we Franciscans had no need for discernment. We took a vow of obedience. We were content to obey, sometimes joyfully, other times less so. We came to understand that our leaders stretched talents that we did not even realize we possessed. These talents then were used to minister to those to whom we were sent.

We came to a new understanding of obedience during the years of the Second Vatican Council especially with the passage of *Perfectae Caritatis* which had a profound impact upon our lives. It particularly impacted our understanding of the vowed life. Obedience became active according to the document from Vatican II. This necessitated discernment on the part of all involved in the decision making process, both leaders and subjects, though we Franciscans always avoided those terms for we were called to be brothers and sisters. Ecclesial structures vied with fraternal structures.

Obedience was now tied to discernment which began with a prayerful listening experience for all involved in our life choices and decisions. Gradually there were seminars, workshops and articles on Franciscan discernment. But true to form for Franciscans, we realized one size did not fit all, so then various styles of discernment were employed.

In the spirit of Francis and Clare, though, there were certain givens, certain suppositions in any form of Franciscan discernment. First and foremost, it must involve the Word of God both written and lived. It must also consider the gifts and graces we have received and so were called to use for ourselves and others.

Pope Francis, as a faithful Jesuit but with a Franciscan heart in both word and example, has given us insights into discernment. In an address to those in consecrated life delivered on the occasion of the Feast of the Presentation he raised the question: 'What moves you?' The question gives us pause. For some of us nothing has moved us in a long time. We live structured lives which can often get stale. Stale bread cannot be blessed, broken and distributed, which is our responsibility in ministering to the People of God.

Speaking of Simeon, he says that he was moved by the Spirit, the essential Person in any discernment process. This is a call to be open to the movement within us by the Spirit; Simeon saw salvation, we need to identify what is necessary for us to be saved from and for what we are being saved; and Simeon takes the child into his arms, reminiscent for us of St Anthony of Padua holding the Child in his arms with the Child balanced on the Book of Life, our central text in discernment.

Discernment is the search for a direction, an answer. Pope Francis observes: 'That is what the Holy Spirit does: He enables us to discern God's presence and activity not in great things, in outward appearances or shows of force, but in littleness and vulnerability.'

# Introduction

I am reminded of that poignant passage in Léon Bloy's long forgotten but wisdom filled novel *The Woman Who Was Poor* in which Clotilde, the poor woman of the title, goes to Mass concerned about how she will pay her upcoming rent. She was overjoyed when she heard the Gospel of the two debtors proclaimed. Now she thought the preacher will speak of the ungrateful debtor whose debts were forgiven but he would not forgive his own debtors. But the preacher did not preach that sermon at all. The people did not hear that Gospel explained. Her vulnerability deepens.

Poverty is essential to any Franciscan discernment process, not a poverty of things but a poverty of being, of vulnerability. We need grace to proceed as did Francis and Clare so many times in their lives when they did not know where to turn. Discernment was a way of life for them. Pope Francis warns us against 'a naïve gaze [that] flees reality and refuses to see problems. A sapiential gaze can look within and see beyond.'

Then there is also Pope Francis' new emphasis on synodality which is a new structure for a listening church: we must listen to the living Word of God vibrant in our hearts and minds, mull it over with the written Word of God so that we might encounter the Word of God himself in our lives. We are called to do this together. We in Franciscan Life are called to synodality in our own structures.

For a Franciscan the discerning person is far more important than the method of discernment. The person must accept his or her own poverty when entering the process, must seek to have a listening heart and an alert mind, relying on the grace of God in his or her pursuit. Then a methodology is important lest the person simply wander aimlessly in unknown fields.

# Journeying toward Wisdom

In this work I propose that we follow St Bonaventure's *Collations on the Seven Gifts of the Holy Spirit*,[1] focusing on each gift given to us by the Holy Spirit as we pursue life in Christ. Each gift offers a unique opportunity to live a gifted life. However, as we pursue such a path, it is important to allow freedom to the discerning person to linger at length or briefly. A gift given should be a gift used at the discretion of the discerning person who must carefully discern whether this is an avoidance technique or that an issue has been adequately pursued previously. There is an enormous difference. I must not avoid a gift but I may pass over one which has already been utilized.

My main attraction to this commentary by St Bonaventure is that it is founded on the fundamental Franciscan value of poverty. In his introduction Bonaventure makes it clear that what attracts God to us is not our perfection but our imperfection which needs healing. What a twist of theology; what a coincidence of opposites. Bonaventure tells us that it is this imperfection that is made whole through the gifts of the Holy Spirit. His fundamental text is from James: 'Every good gift and every perfect gift is from above, coming down from the Father of lights.' It is our poverty that makes us attractive to God. It shows we need him. We are not working out our salvation. Salvation is a gift from God. This was the foundation upon which Francis and Clare rebuilt the Church.

So we receive the gifts of the Holy Spirit to guide and direct us through life. It seems sensible then that any Franciscan discernment process should be founded on these gifts.

---

[1] Works of St Bonaventure xiv, *Collations on the Seven Gifts of the Holy Spirit*, introduction and translation by Zachary Hayes OFM, notes by Robert J. Karris OFM (NY: Franciscan Institute Publications, 2008).

# I

# The Gift of Fear of the Lord

No one needs to teach us about fear. A young child waking in the middle of the night senses movement in the darkness. His fear leads to wailing loudly for Mom who rushes in, turns on the light, gives the child a hug and lullabies the babe back to sleep.

As we age, the reality of fear surrounds us. The nightmares are now real. We read of wars in foreign lands and murders on our streets which become part of our daily news. The Church once provided solace but even here we now fear as division surrounds and overwhelms us. We cannot allow ourselves to turn these divisions into inquisitions. We were once involved in inquisitions. Never again.

So when we come to Bonaventurean discernment we wonder at the wisdom of beginning with fear of the Lord. It is a wise decision on Bonaventure's part, however, for if we understand fear of the Lord we will come to understand that we can bring all our fears to the discernment process.

We begin this process with fears that need to be addressed. The fear of the Lord has within itself a cure, a healing power. Fear of the Lord is a gift, a grace from God. The gift is given to heal us by placing all of our fears during the discernment process in God's divine power where mercy also resides.

Power is a dangerous word. We know power hungry people who use their position to destroy others. They too operate out of an all-consuming fear so they make us tremble in our own doubts. God, on the other hand, uses his power to heal us as Bonaventure says: 'God illumines the earthly human being with divine grace and turns that person to the first Principle from whom all things have their origin and by whom they are governed. Then it is that the human person trembles.' Now we tremble in awe of the God who cares for us.

Bonaventure continues: 'What value is there in fearing God? Tobit 4:23 states "Do not be afraid. Indeed, we live a poor life. But if we fear God, we will have many good things"'. Once again Bonaventure appeals to our poverty of being, a constant Franciscan theme. This process opens us to the influence of divine grace, which is the very purpose of a Franciscan oriented discernment process.

Recently, a dear friend and poet Sr Fran McManus RSM, sent me this poem based on Luke 13:10–17, a passage that clearly contrasts the power of the Scribes and Pharisees who value laws over persons and the power of Jesus who values compassion over obedience to the law, as Bonaventure makes clear in his *Commentary on the Gospel of Luke*.

The poem reads:

> Jesus, I remember when the demon left…
> My spine straightened after eighteen long years,
> freed, healed, and yet feeling almost bereft
> my surprised gratitude mixes with new fears
> Mine had become others' story to tell.
> From safe distance they'd throw coins and food
> to the evil woman under demon's spell.
> Can they or I trust this is change for good?
> For so many years, I had been bowed down,

my world view shrunk to fit a child's line of sight,
if seen, lower than a bug on the ground.
Took me a while, Jesus, to give up the fight.
First stricken, I longed to see the sky.
Enough now to be reflected in your eye.

See how the poet captures the experience of discerning. Our demons, our fears have disappeared. There is a sense of relief, of freedom and of gratitude. Yet there are lingering new fears. Discernment is never ending. Once begun it must continue throughout our lives to deal with new fears: 'Can they or I trust this is change for good?' The poem ends though with great relief and satisfaction: 'Enough now to be reflected in your eye.' What a wonderful way to remind us that Love casts out all fear.

POVERTY

# II

# The Gift of Piety

If we are to appreciate Bonaventure's understanding of the gift of piety, we must begin with chapter eight of the *Legenda Maior* in which Bonaventure expounds on the affectionate piety of St Francis, for in that chapter he presents piety not devotionally but relationally: It is piety 'that drew him to God through devotion, transformed him into Christ through compassion, attracted him to his neighbour through self-emptying and symbolically revealed a return to the state of original innocence though universal reconciliation'. Put simply, it means that our relationships echo life in the Trinity. Francis experienced the Father through a devotion to him. This spirit of devotion is not a prayer book of many prayers but rather it is a deeply held and felt love: Francis was devoted to the Father. He was transformed, not simply converted, but made into Christ to be eucharist for those he encountered and touched which attracted him to others because, like Christ coming among us, he was emptied of self and filled with original innocence. This is not only astonishing praise of one saint for another but it also shows that Bonaventure was devoted to Francis.

The gift of piety which is given to us as we discern our future must ring true with the elements described by Bonaventure for Francis. Not to the extent that Francis possessed them but nevertheless they are our aim and goal in the discernment process; our devotion to the Father, desire to be transformed into Christ for our world and emptying ourselves for the sake of others establishes our Franciscan approach to discernment. Franciscan discernment is never oriented toward the self. It opens us to our relationship with the Trinity, with one another and with all of creation.

Of course, all relationships can become problematic in life, especially our relationship with God, with self and with others. We must begin then by looking carefully at these relationships. Which are in good order? Which are in need of the touch of the Spirit? Which are shattered?

First we look at our relationship with God for if that is disordered all our relationships will be disordered. Bonaventure points out to us that 'the exercise of piety consists of three acts: the reverence of divine worship, the guarding of interior holiness, and the superabundance of interior compassion'.

The question for Bonaventure and even for Francis and Clare was never how often do you worship. Rather, it is how well do you worship. During a discernment process our times of worship do not need to be frequent but they must be sincere acts of worships. Bonaventure says, 'Job tells us that piety is the worship of God … The worship of God consists above all in reverence for God.'

This simply put means worship and reverence are essential to any process of discernment. This process leads us to reflect time and again about our relationship with God.

We move on knowing that we will return time and again to be sure that God is still travelling with us. We need to turn to our 'interior holiness', that is, 'No one can have an attitude of peace himself without possessing peace … The tranquillity of peace' is found in the tranquillity of conscience.

This is a rare moment for Bonaventure for he turns from being the fine spiritual writer that he is to being a fine psychologist, stating that to proceed you must be on good terms with yourself. That tranquillity only comes with a clear conscience. He uses few words to convey so very much. If we are going to enter into a discernment process, we must know ourselves. Not the self we project but the self that we truly are. Yes, we know there are many selves in each one of us but unless there is a core self, there are only many selves, not one united self.

If the thought has crossed your mind that maybe, just maybe, the old notion of obedience wasn't so bad after all, you are not alone. This appears to be a massive task except that we are given the gift of piety, the grace to look at God and ourselves and to discover that we indeed are good.

Having made that discovery we look at others for whom Bonaventure calls for a 'superabundance of interior compassion'. No doubt he has in mind the many episodes in the life of Francis in which he shows compassion toward his weaker brothers.

Among these others are those who are journeying with us through this process. Perhaps they include a spiritual guide, members of our leadership teams, close friends who are also our confidantes. Each has a unique role to play. The spiritual guide is one who knows us spiritually better than most. They are significant but we must always remember that their knowledge of us comes from us which also indicates its limitations. The leadership team members are also important but often they have agendas such as 'filling slots' which are important for the institution but not always for the individual. They are the ones though who often stretch us, as I noted earlier, helping us to see our talents that are not being used.

The confidantes may prove most valuable because they know us the best. We need all of them to make discernment move beyond self-concern.

Then there are those to whom we minister and those to whom we may be called to minister in the future. What effect does any decision we make have on these people, especially those who have placed their trust in us?

The poet Jason Allen-Paisant offers us another possibility. In a book of poetic memoir *Self-Portrait as Othello*, Othello becomes 'the prism through which my story is refracted', as the author puts it, interplaying the struggles of Othello with his own.

Who among the mystical body of Christ would we chose to write our poetic memoir and thus reveal our future? We have an enormous list to choose from. He or she must be a Franciscan who has been a prayer partner through many life struggles and pleasures. Will it be Francis? Clare? Anthony? Agnes? Whoever we choose we begin to see our lives through the eyes of our prayer partner. It can become a mystical experience in itself.

Piety is about relationships. Relationships are necessary for growth. Relationships are always complicated. Piety is the grace that helps us in the 'shape shifting', to use the poet's term, which is so necessary as we discern our life choices within those relationships.

# III

# The Gift of Counsel

As we begin to look at this gift, the thought might occur to you that we have already covered this in the gift of piety. True enough but Bonaventure begins in this refection on counsel with a series of questions which lead us in a new direction: 'Who shall find a valiant woman?' 'Where is wisdom found?' 'Where is the place of understanding?' In true Franciscan form, he responds; in 'the most blessed glorious Virgin'. He not only calls us to turn to Mary but unites his desire that we do so both with Scripture and the prayers of Francis who greets her in his *Salutations*:

> Hail, O Lady, Holy Queen,
> Mary, holy Mother of God:
> you are the virgin made church
> and the one chosen by the most holy Father in heaven
> whom he consecrated with his most holy beloved Son
> and with the Holy Spirit the Paraclete,
> in whom there was and is
> all the fullness of grace and every good!
> And, hail all you holy virtues
> which through the grace and light of the Holy Spirit

are poured into the hearts of the faithful
so that from their faithless state
you may make them faithful to God.

While I have edited the prayer, I have done so to emphasize what Bonaventure emphasizes in his writings on Mary. First, Francis addresses her as the Mother of God, not simply the Mother of Jesus. There is a union between Mary and God that no other creature can ever possess but can only participate in.

Then there is the marvellous phrase Virgin made Church. Mary is the church who brings her Son to the world. This becomes a fundamental belief for followers of Francis. When he rebuilds the church he does so that all the pomposity should disappear and reveal the poor Christ. Once again it reveals the very purpose of our poverty: to see him more clearly.

To accomplish this we become aware of the fullness of grace and goodness so all the virtues become present to us, as Bonaventure will make clear, emphasizing that discernment is about faithfulness to God. Bonaventure makes this the centre of his presentation on the Gift of Counsel noting that we turn to her 'for the discernment of her saving counsel'. Bonaventure wants to situate Mary's saving counsel within the framework of three types of counsel: right reason, good will, and virtue.

When using right reason in the discernment process, one must ask three questions: Is it permitted? Is it appropriate? Is it expedient? Bonaventure rightly cautions us that many things that are permitted may not be appropriate in given times, places and personalities. If we discern that it is both permissible and appropriate, we still need to discern whether or not it is expedient. Perhaps a better word would be prudent. If we have all three conditions, we can proceed according to right reason.

Another problem arises on our part when we begin to act, once we discern that our actions are reasonable. Reason is not enough. Francis and Clare were not reasonable in their desire to live the Gospel. Many of their actions were beyond reason. They were grace-filled actions.

In a Franciscan setting reasonableness alone is insufficient for action to follow. We recall Bonaventure's words in *De Reductione*: '…to know, to will, and to work constantly with perseverance'. Once we know something, we must then will to do it. The axiom is simple: I know it so I want to do it.

Mary is the exemplar in this process. At the Annunciation she heard and understood Gabriel's message, then she willed that it happen according to his word and it was accomplished. A perfect discernment model, or to quote the title of yet another Bonaventurean work on Mary, we become Mirror[s] of the Blessed Virgin Mary.

Mary never stands alone. She stands with her Son, the perfect counsellor. Neither does Christ stand alone as Bonaventure writes: 'Christ the counsellor has many counsellors with whom he shares his counsel.'

We have many counsellors as we discern our future but none will care for us more than our Mother Mary who, like many a good mother, is by our side throughout the process. Don't ignore her nudges.

OBEDIENCE

# IV

# The Gift of Knowledge

If you wanted to experience the theology of knowledge expounded by St Bonaventure you need only go to St Bonaventure University on a bright, sunny day, lingering a few hours in the University Chapel where you will be surrounded by glorious stained glass windows that present his life. Linger with the colours that shine through each of the enormous windows. You will slowly but almost mystically discover why the Saint, in speaking of the Gift of Knowledge, over and over again uses the word 'radiance' along with 'illumination' to engage us in the discovery of the Franciscan meaning of knowledge.

Since many will be unable to do this, take the story of the Transfiguration recounted in the Gospel of Luke (9:28–36) and commented upon at length in Bonaventure's commentary on that Gospel. While reading Luke's account, reflect on the ambiance that Luke creates. The face of Jesus along with his clothing 'became bright as a flash of lighting'. Then a cloud came, a voice proclaimed 'Listen'.

These scriptural images establish Bonaventure's theology of knowledge as is clear from his observations on the text in his *Commentary on the Gospel of Luke*.

Bonaventure speaks of 'the excellence of the contemplative life … [for] it is full of discernment, devoted dedication, love, security, tranquillity, sweetness and the ability to rise up'. Insisting upon a contemplative stance to attain discernment and the virtues, it requires us 'to rise up' to 'the brightness of Christ's countenance and the radiance of his clothing'.

When we turn to the Gift of Knowledge, we immediately notice the constant repetition of 'radiance' which indicates that radiance is knowledge. Referring to 2 Cor 3:18 he observes: 'All of us reflecting as in a mirror the glory of the Lord with faces unveiled are being transformed into his very image from radiance to radiance as through the Spirit of the Lord. The radiance of the Lord is knowledge.'

Further he writes: 'The gift of God is the knowledge of grace. And the knowledge of glory is not only a gift but also a reward … God is the Lord of all knowledge.'

This is based upon his theology of illumination which stands in direct opposition to the *Tabula Rasa* theory of knowledge held by other Scholastics. Bonaventure claims we are born with infused knowledge.

Returning for a moment to the University Chapel, we notice that as the sun comes through the windows the colours attract our attention. Moving slowly, we see things differently. The colours change. So do our insights. We are experiencing Bonaventure's theology of illumination.

Bonaventure tells us that there are three kinds of truth: the truth of reality, the truth of speech and the truth of morals. But it is Sacred Scripture that unites them all: 'Sacred Scripture is compared to the water of the sea because of the depths of its mysteries and the multiplicity of its meanings.'

This is a stunning image to be aware of as we continue our journey through the discernment process. It is not enough for us to find proof texts for our positions and desires. We must be bathed in the Word of God so it seeps into our very being until that being radiates with the truth discovered through an illuminated heart.

Discernment, then, is not fact finding even though facts may be important. Rather it is being saturated by the Word of God until the Truth is revealed to us.

Bonaventure provides us with a final warning though: 'Knowledge puffs up but charity builds up. One must join charity with knowledge so that a person might have both knowledge and charity at the same time.' Said like the true Franciscan that he is. We must always be rooted and grounded in love.

# V

# The Gift of Understanding

In the *Legenda Maior*, chapter six, St Bonaventure extols the humility of St Francis calling this virtue 'the guardian of all the virtues'. It should come as no surprise then that when he introduces the gift of understanding, he tells us that there is a need for humility in order to receive this gift: 'This gift demands that a person be grateful to God. It also brings about that a person comes to know himself in a new way, together with the gift and the source of the gift.'

What Bonaventure is demanding is that knowledge becomes understanding. There is a need to accept understanding as a gift from God not as a result of a personal search. This requires humble acceptance of the gift as gift which then become a life of gratitude to God.

This raises several questions in the discerning process: Do I believe myself to be in control of my life and its decisions? If so, I could simply go my own way and decide for myself. If not, then I must accept Bonaventure's consequence, 'a person comes to know himself in a new way'. That way, of course, is that I do not belong to myself nor does the life that I live now with baptismal, and for many of us consecrated, promises.

This raises yet another question: have we unknowingly become so secularized that the secular world not our religious world controls our decisions? We cannot continue the discernment process without grappling with these questions.

It is urgent that we remember that our God is not an authoritarian God who has predetermined our lives for us. Bonaventure writes: 'It is God's pleasure to accept what we do, approving it in the present, and rewarding it in the future.' Incredibly we have a God who trusts us. Too often we ask the wrong question. It is not what does God want me to do. We already know the answer to that question and in fact pray it every day several times, 'Thy kingdom come, thy will be done'. His will is the coming of the Kingdom. How we are to do that is our choice. The catch is we must understand the choice is for his Kingdom, not ours.

There is still a question concerning understanding that remains for us to consider. Jesus himself asks it in John 12:12–15:

> When he had finished washing their feet, he put on his clothes and returned to his place. 'Do you understand what I have done for you?' he asked them. 'You call me teacher' and 'Lord', and rightly so for that is what I am. Now that I, your Lord and Teacher, have washed your feet, you also should wash one another's feet. I have set you an example that you should do as I have done for you.

Jesus, knowing his disciples did not understand, spelled it out for them. They were to make decisions based on the needs of one another, not simply on what is good for themselves. In discerning it is important to understand this call to charity, to look after one another, caring for one another.

Like many religious today, I live in a retirement fraternity. There are about thirty of us at any given time. We have all known one another for the most part for fifty or sixty years. Of course, we have stories to tell! Yet no one need encourage us to care for one another. We simply do it. It is not overwhelming. We simply do it. No need to wash one another's feet annually. We do it daily. Some days the only thing I can say is I understand.

Knowing leads to understanding; both gifts are given for daily life and for use in a Franciscan discernment process. It will clarify issues as we search for a resolution to the issue that led in into discernment.

# VI

# The Gift of Fortitude

In approaching Bonaventure's conferences on fortitude, we find that there is an evening conference and a morning conference the next day. Quite honestly, the evening conference has little to offer us. Bonaventure writes of the need for fortitude in the face of war. We are the warriors. It's hardly an appealing contemporary image.

The morning conference dealing once again with Mary begins rather slowly until Bonaventure stops theologizing and turns to images of Mary, all fresh, and at least from my point of view, never heard of before.

Referring to Psalm 86 which speaks of Zion but which Bonaventure applies to Mary: 'the commandments of God are in the heart of a holy woman, that is, the glorious virgin … these commandments of God were established in her heart.' In other words, while Moses carried stone tablets with the commandments written on them, the Virgin Mary carried them in her heart. She lived them presenting them to us. The imitation of Mary here is that we too must learn to carry the commandments within our hearts, making them our desired way to behave toward God, one another and ourselves.

Moving on, Bonaventure speaks of how Eve destroyed the house that God gave them but Mary rebuilt that house. No Franciscan can miss the point here. Francis too was called to rebuild the church but had a slow start because he misinterpreted it. Mary acted immediately. We too are more like Francis so we need to overcome the false starts we make in rebuilding the church until with the grace of the Holy Spirit we find our appropriate way.

While the third image should be obvious to us, we miss it because we pray without thinking 'the Holy Spirit will come upon you and the Most High will overshadow you'. Mary is the new Ark of the Covenant, overshadowed to reveal the presence of God in our midst. The Ark lives among the people as Mary chose to do. We too must strive to be among the people to reveal the Lord to them in their daily struggles and to allow them to reveal the Lord to us in our struggles.

And yet another image: 'Since the love of God burned in a special way in the spirit of the Virgin, she therefore accomplished wonderful things in her flesh … The bush was on fire but was not consumed.' For Bonaventure she was the burning bush enflamed with God's love. We are also called to reveal the love of God to one another so that others discover in who we are the love we carry for the Lord and them.

These are telling images that Bonaventure applies to the Virgin Mary because each one shows his appreciation for her role among us and in any discernment process. We need to spend time in discernment to discern the primary image of Mary we will carry in us as we prepare to enter a new phase of our discernment process.

Bonaventure insists we need another gift to accomplish that. In the first conference on Fortitude he writes, 'the gift of fortitude is the serene solace of hope … hold the hope set before you.'

It is difficult for us to be hopeful in this hopeless age. We try. We enter into our world in the belief that our hope will make a difference. We know in our hearts that it is only a dream, a wish at best. This hope that will not leave us alone, though, is not simply human hope. It is the gift of hope urging us not to give up. Hope is more than a feeling. It is a virtue, a gift from God to view reality differently than many of our neighbours who have given up hope.

Bonaventure also identifies Mary as our hope adding that 'the whole Christian people is begotten from the womb of the glorious Virgin'.

No doubt Francis, Clare and the other brothers and sisters rejoice in the newly articulated identity Mary has been given by Bonaventure.

Our task during this time of discernment is to work with the images and virtues that must become a part of our daily lives wherever discernment leads us.

CHASTITY

# VII

# The Gift of Wisdom

In considering the Gift of Wisdom, Bonaventure provides us with a surprising conclusion to the study of the Gifts of the Holy Spirit as well as to our discernment process. It does get a bit cumbersome because of the various images that the Saint uses so we shall forego the images and present his conclusions. Or perhaps we should say inclusions because Bonaventure includes all of the virtues and gifts we have investigated and more in wisdom. In other words, if you are wise, you have a spattering of them all. This surely follows the lead of St Francis who in the *Salutation of the Virtues* presents the virtues as brothers and sisters to demonstrate that the relationships among the virtues work together for the good of the soul.

It may come as a surprise that Bonaventure seems so contemporary in his opening lines about the gift of wisdom when he says: 'if you desire wisdom, then seek justice' for we live in a world that seeks justice but has little wisdom, so we have neither. For the Seraphic Doctor they are intrinsically united.

We often miss the connection because the wisdom that we seek is self-serving, a wisdom that serves our advantages because 'we have a high regard for an abundance of wealth but Christ chose poverty'. We seek justice in our care for others to gain a wisdom. Bonaventure cautions us: 'Christ died to do away with and destroy vain wisdom, he rose and ascended in order to teach true wisdom and to confirm it in our hearts.' Rejecting the wisdom of the world, we accept the gift of wisdom from the Holy Spirit.

Bonaventure then outlines some other virtues to be included in wisdom. What is useful for us are the virtues which he accumulates for a wise person to conclude and include in an ongoing discernment process.

First there is *purity* which guides us to treat all persons with the respect and dignity of being a person rather than an object. When we make a person an object of our lust — so easily done in our world, especially in advertising — we turn those persons into objects. Humility is necessary to treat the other as an equal in dignity no matter his or her status life. This is a call to treat each person as a person worthy of our care and respect.

Another virtue is *patience*. Bonaventure quotes Proverbs 24:29: 'One who is patient is governed by much wisdom … one who is impatient takes delight in his folly and thus destroys the house of wisdom he is trying to build.' It is easy for us to demand that people be patient with us. It is not so easy for us to be patient with others, especially when we want answers. Discernment is not about convincing others to be patient with us. It is about our learning to be patient with ourselves even when answers are not staring us in the face.

The next virtue is *minding our speech*. Silence is essential to any search for wisdom in discernment. We should not babble pointlessly and endlessly because we will then miss the whispers of the Spirit. Bonaventure offers this insight:

'Silence and wisdom are so closely related that if a fool were to maintain silence, he would be considered wise.'

*Kindness and generosity* are often just seen as good manners instead of virtues. They play an essential role in wisdom-seeking. Bonaventure believes, and we concur, that a kind and generous person finds it easier to persuade us than an angry person who rails against us. Yet we often use anger more readily when we become frustrated but then we are frustrating the discernment process.

Wisdom then is an all-inclusive gift of the Holy Spirit. While we may need to look at individual aspects of wisdom as we discern, eventually it will be enough to seek wisdom. Isn't this the moment for which we were waiting? Isn't it what Francis learned when he cried out in *The Salutations of the Virtues*: 'Hail, Queen Wisdom'?

Let us conclude with this powerful prayer of St Bonaventure which can be a *vademecum* to always keep in mind and heart all we have said, noting that Bonaventure reaffirms the primacy of wisdom by beginning with that virtue and allowing the other virtues to flow from the wisdom we have gained through discernment.

## ST BONAVENTURE'S PRAYER FOR THE
## SEVEN GIFTS OF THE HOLY SPIRIT

We pray the most merciful Father,
through you, his only-begotten Son,
made man for us, crucified and glorified,
that he send us from his treasures
the Spirit of sevenfold grace
who rested upon you in all fullness.

The spirit, that is, of wisdom,
that we may savour the life-giving taste
of the fruit of the Tree of Life, which you truly are;

the gift of understanding,
which enlightens the insights of our mind;

the gift of counsel,
whereby we may set out on our journey
along right paths,
following in your footsteps;

the gift of fortitude,
through which we may overcome
the violent assaults of the Enemy;

the gift of knowledge,
by which we may be filled with the brilliance
of your sacred teaching to discern good from evil;

the gift of piety,
that we may clothe our heats with mercy;

the gift of fear,
whereby, drawing away from all evil,
we may be at peace
in the reverential love of your eternal Majesty.

For you have willed us to ask for these things
in that holy prayer you taught us;
so now we implore them of you
through your holy cross
and to the praise of your most holy name.

To whom, with the Father and the Holy Spirit,
be all honour and glory,
thanksgiving, splendour and power
for ever and ever. Amen.[1]

---

[1] Translation from *The Tree of Life* (*Lignum Vitae* 49) by Eric Doyle OFM, first published in *The Tablet* (6 June 1974), 567.

# Introduction to Part II

## SPIRITUAL DIRECTION

When a person begins discernment, it should be obvious that the best person to journey with the discerning person is one's spiritual director since the director already has a unique relationship with the directee.

This relationship is seasoned by inner concerns in daily living and time. Together the person discerning involves his or her director to consider one's overall spiritual well-being in the context of daily lived experience. The choices made along that journey impact the new choices presented in discernment which demand an entrance into the journey toward wisdom.

In an effort to provide some assistance about this relationship, we present here three articles that may prove helpful in assessing the condition of one spiritual direction experience.

The first article uses the relationship between Francis and Leo as a model to use in Franciscan spiritual direction while the second article uses a particular case to use in measuring the adequacy of direction. It aims to focus on an atmosphere of caring, non-judgmental concern showing the vast difference between confession, which is a moral assessment, and spiritual direction which seeks to discover God's presence in all of life's experiences.

A third article deals with those of us who are elderly, which is the vast number of us in religious life today. Our needs and concerns are not only physically different than they were when we were more active but also our spiritual and theological concerns which have necessarily been transformed over time.

It is our hope in presenting this section that it will assist a person to integrate spiritual direction into the discernment process.

# On the Road with Francis and Leo

The novelist Cormac McCarthy who according to some critics has journeyed from agnosticism to a recovery of transcendence, seems to have become obsessed about what happens on the road. First there was his apocalyptic novel *The Road* in which a father and son travel through the devastated land in search of food, shelter and safety; followed now by the twin novels *The Passenger* and *Stella Maris* which are about a brother and sister obsessed by physics and mathematics as they search for meaning along the road.

*The Road* has been interpreted by critics differently. Some see it as pessimistic proclaiming the end of reality as we know it. Others interpret it as optimistic as the young boy is the only survivor poised to carry on the future of the world.

Stories on the road also fill the Gospels, none more memorable than the story of Emmaus. Two depressed disciples give up hope as they return home after the crucifixion of Jesus until a stranger joins them updating them on the latest happenings in the Jesus story. This revives their hope.

The story of Francis and Leo, as discovered in the letter to Leo, is similar to both the McCarthy account as well as the Emmaus account. The letter begins simply enough: a brother addresses his brother but Brother Francis seems to address

Brother Leo with concerns. He wishes him 'Health and Peace'. This is no mere physical health. Francis immediately includes Peace. It is easy to see in these juxtaposed terms a relationship: Francis is concerned about Leo's mental and spiritual well-being, so much so that Francis immediately changes the terms under which he writes to Leo. He addressed Leo as a mother to her son. He did not change it to be more natural as a father to a son but rather the more affectionate term for Francis: mother. Francis' own relationship to his father and mother was conflicted. After his conversion, his father was not kind to him while his mother remained the loving mother she always was. This is a loving relationship.

Then comes the telling line, 'I am putting before you everything we said on the road'. Our initial reaction to these words is quite simply that we would like to know what they talked about along the road. We already know, for Francis reminds Leo: 'in whatever way it seems better to you to please the Lord God and to follow his footprint and poverty, do it with the blessing of the Lord God and my obedience.' This is not new advice to Leo. It is a repetition of what he had said along the road but in more precise and clearer words.

First Francis reiterates his trust in Leo: 'In whatever way it seems better to you.' Francis as a mother does not tell Leo what to do. He affirms his own discerning heart. So Francis only gives advice and his obedience is an affirmation of what Leo has come to but Francis presents three conditions; it pleases the Lord God, it follows in the footprints of Jesus, and it remains true to his love of poverty. Francis does not present himself as the mediator of God. Rather he advises Leo to be attentive to the will of God while permitting Jesus to provide the footprints to follow along the road with a sense of *sine proprio*, saving nothing for himself. His final words are as motherly as he began: 'If you need and want to, come', uniting necessity and desire 'for the sake of your soul and consolation'.

I know of no better map for spiritual guidance than this letter of Francis to Leo. Often, the guide and the guided are already in a relationship so it necessitates a change in the relationship when the guide decides to accept a person for guidance. This needs to be attended to at the beginning of the process.

This new relationship, though, is not a power relationship. It is a loving relationship of daughter to mother or son to mother. The guide does not and cannot put his or her agenda on the guided. Rather, with patience and gentleness, one accompanies the son or daughter on his or her journey always following the advice of Francis to Leo with the will of God and the footprints of Jesus being the road map for the spiritual journey.

We turn now to Cormac McCarthy's latest novel *Stella Maris*. The main character is Alicia, mentally suffering she admits herself once again to this hospital where she and her therapist basically talk about mathematics in which Alicia finds meaning and escape from her reality. Dr Cohen is patient as he works to save her from suicide. At the conclusion of the novel she tells Dr Cohen:

> I'd hike into the mountains. Stay off the road … I'd have a canteen for water for when the time came that I was too weak to move about. After a while the water would taste extraordinary. It would taste like music. I'd wrap myself in the blanket at night against the cold and watch the bones take shape beneath my skin and I would pray that I might see the truth of the world before I died. Sometimes at night the animals would come to the edge of the fire and move about and their shadows would move among the trees and I would understand that when

the last fire was ashes they would come and carry
me away and I would be their eucharist. And that
would be my life.

This is a foretelling of her suicide which is revealed in the
companion novel *The Passenger*.

Her longing to be devoured, to be eucharist, is not possible,
however, because she seems quite incapable of appropriate
relationships. Her Gnostic pessimism frequently reveals itself
in the therapy sessions, never more clearly than when she says
'the world has created no living thing it does not intend to
destroy'. We enter her world of theological starvation.

Bonaventure does help us to guide the empty soul, the
hungry soul, the soul in darkness, the soul bound in want or
is in iron in his work *On the Most Holy Body of Christ*. He points
out that when dealing with those we guide in these seeming
maladies of the soul, the guide must be cautious so that he or
she guides the person through the stages of spiritual growth
without imposing solutions upon the guided who should be
led to discover such solutions for him or herself.

Often we will encounter people who feel empty because
they no longer believe that God dwells within them or they
hunger for the Bread of Life yet feel unworthy so they sit in
darkness, in the shadow of spiritual death. Often enough the
guide listens with one ear while with the other is listening for
solutions to these 'problems'. But spiritual guides are not
problem solvers. Rather they are there like Virgil leading
Dante through hell. They travel with the depressed soul as
together they search for the light that shines in the darkness.

In my early days of being introduced to Franciscan
spirituality, we were told to always remember that our
spirituality could be summarized in the three Cs: the crib, the
ciborium, and the cross. The crib is the symbol that
emphasizes the centrality of the Incarnation in Franciscan

spirituality and theology. The ciborium points us to the importance of the Eucharist emphasized in our daily lives. It is unfortunate though that very often the cross which unites our suffering to the suffering of Christ has disappeared in much Franciscan thought today. It is frequently the most heartfelt aspect of Franciscan spirituality for so many of our people. We must assist the guided to search for the true cross within themselves. It is not the crosses we take up as penances. It is not the crosses that others unwittingly place on our shoulders. We search for the true cross within ourselves for we are our own heaviest cross. We help those we guide to not be afraid to take up this cross and bear it until they learn to die and be resurrected daily. This experience transforms the guided into their true self. Together the crib, ciborium and cross form the core of our Franciscan spiritual lives.

There are occasions when the guide is tempted to become a therapist, especially when he or she deals with the crosses in the life of those we guide. The guide needs to be alert to his or her inability to provide such help and recommend a caring therapist. Oftentimes the guide and therapist work together to assist the guided person never making the guided feel abandoned by the guide. Mothers never abandon their children.

Persons who identity their true desires by their wants are, according to Bonaventure, persons 'in iron', that is, their wants bind them making their hearts hardened to spiritual desires. The conundrum here is that a person arrives for guidance because he or she wants to be holy. The compassionate guide understands this desire but gently helps the guided to learn that it is what God wants that matters. It is no easy task to help a person move from 'I want' to 'God wants' but it is a necessary one.

In such a case, it is always helpful to turn to the authentic prayers of St Francis which frequently decentre the self in favour of centring us on Christ. Perhaps the prayer written for Brother Leo would be most appropriate.

> You are holy, Lord, the only God,
>> and your deeds are wonderful.
> You are strong.
>> You are great.
>> You are the Most High.
>> You are almighty.
>> You, Holy Father are King of heaven and earth.
> You are Three and One,
>> Lord God, all Good.
>> You are Good, all Good, supreme Good,
>> Lord God, living and true.
> You are love,
>> You are wisdom.
>> You are humility,
>> You are endurance.
>> You are rest,
>> You are peace.
>> You are joy and gladness.
>> You are just and moderation.
>> You are all our riches,
>> and you suffice for us.
> You are beauty.
>> You are gentleness.
>> You are our protector,
>> You are our guardian and defender.
>> You are our courage.
>> You are our haven and hope.
> You are our faith,
>> Our great consolation.
>> You are our eternal life,

# On The Road with Francis and Leo

> Great and wonderful Lord,
> God Almighty,
> Merciful Saviour.[1]

Sometimes when we read this prayer, we think that Francis is just putting together all the positive adjectives he recalls. Then we miss the point. Francis is creating a prayer to accompany his letter. Francis, Leo's mother, is introducing his Father to Leo, a Father who is his guardian and defender, strength and endurance, riches and courage, great and merciful. Leo now has a mother and father who are his everything, considering that his mother was poor but his father was rich. What a genius the Poverello was in dealing with Leo. We might even dare to say that he made a far better spiritual guide than a leader of the Movement he started.

When we look at this relationship between Francis and Leo seeking greater union with Jesus and the Father, we begin to understand the role of the Holy Spirit in the entire process. It is the grace of the Spirit that permeates every relationship which seeks the Lord on the road and in spiritual guidance.

Bonaventure tells us in his *Commentary on the Gospel of Luke* that it is hospitality that showed the two discouraged disciples the true identity of the stranger who joined them. As Jesus seemed to be walking on, it was they who invited him to dine with them, to linger awhile as they drank in the meaning of all that he told them that led to the recognition of Jesus' true identity.

Hospitality must always be the atmosphere of Franciscan spiritual guidance, as mother and daughter, mother and son sit to discover their true identity in Christ.

---

[1] 'The Praises of God', *Omnibus*, 125–26. See bibliography for full details.

# Attending Our Wound

Several years ago when I was doing spiritual guidance in New York City I also taught a course on St Bonaventure's *Tree of Life*.[1] There were twenty-five to thirty participants on the course. At the end of each session I would ask the participants to put their reactions on an index card. After six weeks I had accumulated a number of index cards, all long gone save for one. That one was from a young lady whom I was also guiding on her spiritual journey. The card reads: 'I had always felt that Bonaventure had a passionate relationship with Jesus. The way Bonaventure writes, it's as if he wants to come up with hundreds of reasons to fall in love with Jesus — like he's stoking his heart to "feel" Jesus.' Those words were written at the end of the class where we discussed LV39,[2] a rather dense exposition of Pentecost. I was very moved by her insight so that in our next spiritual guidance session I began by commenting on it. It became the source of several meetings that followed.

The particular section is titled 'Jesus Giver of the Spirit'. Bonaventure begins rather prosaically recounting the events

---

[1] Classics of Western Spirituality, *Bonaventure:The Soul's Joureny into God; The Tree of Life; The Life of St Francis,* trans. by Ewert Cousins (NY: Paulist Press, 1978).

[2] Ibid.,163.

of the first Pentecost, including that Mary was there, though as we know he also makes clear that she had already received the Spirit at the Annunciation. Why then was she there? The most human response is that Jesus had given John the task of caring for Mary so he would insist on Mary staying nearby. There is, however, a more profound meaning. Mary was there to greet her Spouse, the Holy Spirit, to assure the fulfilment of this latest descent of the Spirit.

This relationship between John and Mary mirrors the relationship that exists between the spiritual guide and the guided person furthering the awareness of the Holy Spirit along with the duties that come with such a descent. After all, it was not enough for Mary when she learned that the Holy Spirit descended upon her and dwelt within her then to travel to Elizabeth. Only then did she sing her Magnificat. The poet Drew Jackson puts it so well in his poem *That Girl Can Sing*:

*Go on, Mary!*

Bless our ears with your sonic theology
Lift us up with your melodic doctrine.
Magnify! Magnify!
This voice is magnificent.[3]

The disciples 'are given speech' to 'their mouth'. The singular indicates that Bonaventure wants us to know that their message was unified. In turn it 'taught them the truth, aided by his grace'. Every word of Bonaventure must be attended to. The disciples were called to speak not their truth but the Truth who was revealed to them because of the grace which they received from the Holy Spirit. They are not concerned with self-reflection or even worse with self-discovery. Rather, they are concerned with the message revealed which is now to be promulgated to everyone in whatever language the

---

[3] Drew Jackson, *God Speaks Through Wombs* (Il, Downers Grove: InterVarsity Press, 2021),17.

listeners spoke. They did not receive the grace of Pentecost simply for themselves.

This process becomes our Pentecost process at our confirmation. It is renewed throughout our lives. Spiritual guidance is one means given to us to assure this ongoing process.

Bonaventure adds though that the tongues of fire are also given 'to give light to the intellect', carefully including the entire person: affect and intellect. To be too affective is to deny the intellectual side of our being but conversely to be too intellectual is to deny that we have an affect. Both are God-given. Balanced we are 'inflamed with love and illumined by his teaching'. The result then is 'ardour, virtue and power', all the gifts of Pentecost, moving as always with the Seraphic Doctor through the stages of purgation, illumination and union.

We hit a bit of a snag, however, when we turn to the planting of the Church which began at Pentecost because Bonaventure paints a beautiful image of the Church. It is not always our experience, nor has it ever really been, to which even *The Acts of The Apostles* attests. We can easily become disillusioned by what we experience to be Church.

Something happens to our image and expectation of Church. Before we judge, however, we must admit that we are also disillusioned with ourselves. The poet Mary Oliver puts it well in *Don't Hesitate*:

> If you suddenly and unexpectedly feel joy,
> don't hesitate. Give in to it. There are plenty
> of lives and whole towns destroyed or about
> to be. We are not wise, and not very often
> Kind. And much can never be redeemed.
> Still, life has some possibility left. Perhaps this
> is its way of fighting back, that sometimes
> Something happens better than all the riches

> or power in the world. It could be anything,
> but very likely you will notice it in the instant
> when love begins. Anyway, that's often the
> case. Anyway, whatever it is, don't be afraid
> of its plenty. Joy is not made to be a crumb.[4]

Here lies a key to spiritual guidance. The Pentecost experience is not a one-time experience. It happens time and time again on our personal spiritual journey as well as in our ecclesial journeys. The two are closely intertwined. Put simply, where does the personal journeying toward a deeper relationship with God find companionship? Our facile response is in the celebration of the Eucharist. But is it?

As Mary Oliver says 'life has some possibility left'. Take, for example, the young lady who wrote those powerful words with which I began. She does not find her companionship in Eucharistic celebrations, though she loves the Eucharist. She is not alone in her feelings. Crowds are not communities. Spiritual guides do not condemn. They prefer to ask: where then do you find God in your life with others?

She finds church at AA meetings which she attends regularly with people she has come to share the secrets of her life with, without fear of condemnation. She finds these meetings much more satisfying than participating in celebrations that begin with reminding us of our sinfulness.

She has come to understand that there is an enormous difference between mistakes and sins, or as Pope Francis says, our wounds.

The wounded need hospitals. Pope Francis has written extensively on the church as a 'field hospital' as Massimo Borghesi puts it in his book *Catholic Discordance*:

> It is a metaphor that matured through his
> experience of immersion, of incarnation, of

---

[4] Mary Oliver, *Devotions* (NY: Penguin Press, 2017), 61.

coming face to face with the painfully destitute neighbour, materially and spiritually. It comes from Bergoglio's experience of Buenos Aires where he discovered the pain of the world. Succinctly put, the church of Francis is a people's church in a secularized world.[5]

This image is important for the spiritual guide pursuing with the guided person to live in the world in which we find ourselves. The danger though for the guide is to see him or herself as the nurse caring for the wounded. Not so. We need to keep in mind the title of Henri Nouwen's work *The Wounded Healer*. Both the guide and the guided are wounded. In a wholesome relationship they are healing one another. Bonaventure writes:

> In this holy Church which through the wonderful work of the Holy Spirit is diversified in a variety of forms … and yet it is united in a single whole … the Spirit dispenses offices in the church and distributes charismatic gifts. For he himself gave some as disciples, some as prophets, others again as evangelists, others as pastors and teachers … to build up the body of Christ (LV 40).[6]

In guiding others we never paint romantic pictures of life which will disappoint them and even tempt them to forego further journeying. We also avoid helping them to create a 'Jesus and me' spirituality. How easily we forget the call to love God and neighbour. Love is an inclusive experience.

We must help those we guide to discern their role in this church, becoming aware of Bonaventure's updating of the multi-coloured robe of Joseph: 'Then Christ will be clothed

---

[5] Massimo Borghesi, *Catholic Discordance* (MN, Collegeville: Liturgical Press, 2021).

[6] *Bonaventure*,164.

with all the beauty of the elect as if with a many-coloured tunic in which he will shine forth richly adorned as if clothed with all manner of precious stones.[7]

We are told that Confirmation is a one-time sacrament. True enough. Pentecost though is an ongoing life experience through which we discover the precious stone that each one of us is and so want that stone to shine over and over and over to brighten the world which we serve in Jesus' name with the grace of the Holy Spirit. So, in the words of Mary Oliver in her poem *What I have learned so far*: 'Be ignited or be gone!'

---

[7] Ibid., 168.

# Becoming Wise Elders

If we watch the advertisements on TV and read the ads in newspapers and magazines, we would never realize that there are the elderly among us. If we live in any religious order today, however, we realize there are fewer and fewer young people among us. We spend a great amount of time and money trying to attract the young. But what are we doing for the elderly so that their minds and hearts many continue to be formed in the Franciscan image?

Recently, while reading the *Times Literary Supplement*, I came across a review of a book, *The Art of Memoir*. It was not the title or article that attracted my attention. It was the title of the review that caught my eye: 'Be True to Thyself'. Could a Christian accept such an idea? Should I? The elderly have little choice. We have fewer and fewer images of ourselves. For many of us the ones remaining do not even attract us. The elderly, then, need assistance in realizing once again that we are still made in the image and likeness of God; I may be able to repeat it as a mantra. The problem arises when I look at my image of God. Both the self-image of the elderly and the image of God need to be formed once again. Spiritual guidance may be one means of accomplishing that task in elder life.

The elderly may be at a time in life when fears begin to arise about sin and judgment, the afterlife and its many fantasies and meeting God for that horrible cross examination. Often enough the elderly wrestle with God like Jacob. They need a referee in such a wrestling match.

It is of little value, early on at least, to write a history of personal images of God through the years. It may cause more anxiety than healing. Rather than begin with God, it would be more beneficial to begin with the self, using images garnered from the *Life of St Francis* penned by St Bonaventure, who provides us with three images: the leper, the cross, and the lamb. We will examine each one, not that they need to be presented to the one being guided, though they may be but they will primarily assist any guide in helping an elderly person begin to process new fears arising from the aging experience. Bonaventure gives us a fresh look at each one of these images.

While the leper appears in all the accounts of Francis' life as well as in his *Testament*, Bonaventure adds a subtle notion. After giving the leper money and a kiss, Francis mounted his horse and began to ride away. He glanced back 'but though the open plain stretched clear in all directions, he could not see the leper anywhere'. At first, we might wonder: what is the Seraphic Doctor suggesting? Was it really a leper? Was it Christ? For Bonaventure and for us there is no distinction. It is Christ deeply present within the leper.

Elderly people often feel like lepers, outcasts in society, forgotten and ignored, they feel isolated from what was their lives and what has become of them. They do not wear bells, of course, but canes and walkers and now even scooters mark our comings and goings. They readily identify us. Some learn to accept this reality as a given, something they can do little about. Others become saddened by what they perceive as 'abandonment', though family and friends are often there to help. But loneliness becomes the companion of isolation.

I still have lingering thoughts of my father's elderly mother who lived with us. She spoke little English which was one cause of separation. The other was age. When I was too young for school, I remained with her during the day as my parents went off to work and my brother went to school. Most of the day, my grandmother spent sitting at the window, praying the rosary. Even my mother in later life prayed the rosary on her way to and from work. A practice long gone for many of us.

When a person seeking guidance comes to us it is often with questions about God, not companionship with him. In accepting an elderly person for direction, it becomes necessary to assist that person to turn to God to overcome isolation with practices that keep the living God ever present. Each person's practices must be personally developed with the help of the director. No forcing here. No pre-packaged solutions. No magic formulas. Just a director who listens and guides this grace-filled process so that the one being directed, glancing back at life will see what Francis saw: a clear scene on a clear day that speaks of God beyond words and images.

The second image from Bonaventure's *Life of St Francis* is the cross, Christ crucified, an image that recurs over and over again in Bonaventure's rendition of Francis' life. This is significant especially because today we emphasize not the cross but the Incarnation. We need both in our spirituality which is not to say that Christ came to save us through his death and resurrection. His death, like so many things we attributed to God, was caused by our blindness, not by the will of the Father. The cross, though, is an aspect of life. It is especially so as we age. We no longer have need for fasts and Lenten practices. Life itself now provides this free of charge.

What must not be missed here is what Bonaventure says of Francis: 'He carried in his own body the armour of the cross.' The Stigmata. Another sign of identification with Christ. The elderly also carry the armour of the cross in their bodies. I live in a fraternity of retired friars where you hear on any given day, 'I'm not afraid of death. It's the dying process I fear'. We are already in the dying process. Each day reminds us of what was, of what is and of what may be. Dying is in our bones even though we may not be ready to welcome 'Sister Death'. While we consider this a mystical moment in Francis' life, we forget that it took the brothers a strenuous journey to get Francis to where he could proclaim those words. With Francis, though, it is our cross to carry with the help of others and with which we become identified with Christ.

'Carry the seal of the cross', says Bonaventure but we rush from the cross until we realize we are too old to rush anymore, so we have no choice but to surrender to the cross. Embrace what you cannot escape so that the 'bitter becomes sweet'.

Then Bonaventure takes our breath away when he states that Francis had 'the brand-marks of the Lord Jesus'. It is more than an image. For Francis, it was the Stigmata, a gift which brought much discomfort with it. We too are branded by baptism with the marks of Christ. We are then like the lamb branded so to be easily recognized by its owner, who is Christ himself.

So we come to the final image that Bonaventure presents for our reflection. The Seraphic Doctor tells us about a little lamb that Francis gave to Lady Jacoba. She cared for the little creature which became her constant companion even travelling with her to church for Mass.

As we age we can either become lambs or tigers. Some days we are one, some days the other. I know this from experience. We tell stories about the tigers with whom we have lived but we admire the lambs, those who in old age identified with the Lamb of God so that the tiger in us does not lead others to the slaughter.

In her renowned novel *Gilead*, Marilyn Robinson writes, 'when you encounter another person, when you have dealings with anyone at all, it is as if a question is being put to you … What is the Lord asking of me at this moment, in this situation? … If you think this is an emissary sent from the Lord then some benefit is intended for you.' We are back to the leper who is Christ.

In his latest book *The Whole Language*, Gregory Boyle, speaking of the Homeboys for whom he cares, says: 'We don't liberate them. We can only create a place of liberation.' That's Franciscan spiritual guidance in a nutshell. We are called to create a place of liberation for those who come to us. No more burdens. No more scruples. Just Jesus who sets us free.

Boyle also observes that our presumption is that 'it is "content" by mentors that is most compelling'. Not so, he says. 'It is the "context" that matters', which is to say that 'we rarely remember what we've been told but mainly how we were made to feel'. Again a Jesuit making Franciscan sense.

I had an aunt, my favourite, who on turning 85 said to me 'there's a big difference between 80 and 85'. As I now live in my mid-80s, I can attest to the truth of that statement but I also can attest to the fact that I know myself and the Lord much better today than ever before. Some would call it the wisdom of the elderly. Franciscan spiritual guidance should help other elderly people to discover and share that wisdom.

# Appendix

## ARTWORK

Michael Reyes OFM, painter of the artwork in this short volume, has commented that people viewing his art for the first time often note the 'dark' quality of his work. Speaking about the religious vows in particular he notes that: 'The vows, like life, are not always sunny and bright: that is just the perception of them. They are invitations to a deep self-reflection that reveals a nuanced experience that is no different or [more] complicated than any other life.' For him, 'the beauty and power of visual art is that it is capable of going beyond the limitations and precision of words' and as such all viewers' interpretations of his work are 'valid and true'.

In painting these works Michael focused on the feelings evoked in the individual religious when alone at prayer with God, feeling the effects of the vows, which may on the one hand appear to impose limitations, and on the other to set the person free. He finds the image of life compared to a river, as described by John Foley SJ, particularly helpful. He wrote:

> There are two conditions to river life: the first rule
> is that the river must receive its very self from

others. It draws from the high lake, the rains and snows, the estuaries and the oceans. Cut the sources and you dry up the river. Second, a river must at every moment in every way continuously release absolutely everything that it is. A wave must pass its very substance on. It can hold on to nothing at all…
By these two conditions, the river has its self.

Michael explains that this life of constant giving and receiving is captured in his use of both light and dark vertical lines in his work, which represent the reception of life and the giving of new life in a constant cycle. He embraces the difficulties of such a life in his images, rooted as it is in Jesus' teaching that to gain life we must first lose it: 'Like the river, our lives are always on the move, always flowing towards the great sea of our good and loving God.'

Speaking of the religious life Michael says:

In many ways, we religious lose our life in the sense of a private life: we can often feel that we are constantly being watched and are constrained by the expectations of the Church – from parishioners, laypeople, members of the Church hierarchy, even the secular world. On the other hand, we also experience the sometimes lonely process of looking out of the church windows toward those who seek us on the other side, into the 'real' or 'outside' world and can feel left out or out of touch.

To capture this apparent dichotomy, Michael included the windows of a church in each painting – though it is unclear whether one is looking into or out of the church.

# Appendix

The following are Michael's own reflections on the paintings, but he invites each viewer to reflect for themselves on how the vows of religious life speak to their own experience.

## POVERTY

People's first impression of the vow of poverty tends to be that it is the easy one: we'll be taken care of and simply let go of material things. But I've realized after being a friar for ten years that poverty is more than just material things. Poverty can also mean attachment to people: as friars we are called to separate from those we love and to move to where we are needed, not always together. Poverty is learning to let go of both material possessions and those we love, and it is both freeing and difficult. By learning to open ourselves to the practice of giving that which we have back to God, we allow ourselves to be open to receiving new gifts from him as we journey along our path of faith. In this, we are able to offer our whole selves to God and his people in their service, free of those things that might otherwise constrain our ability to serve with abandon or distract our focus from those we seek to serve.

## CHASTITY

Many people who see this piece for the first time often describe it as 'erotic', 'sexual', or 'suggestive', and they ask with some incredulity, 'that is chastity?' I find it interesting that when most people consider the vow of chastity, their first thought is 'no sex!' What I am trying to accomplish with this piece is an invitation to the viewer to look deeply into the image, to look beyond the physicality of the painting and the vow – because there is more to it than genital or romantic pursuit and responses.

The vulnerable and naked figure in the image signifies a complete trust, faith, and vulnerability with God – a total devotion to the very core of our being. By extension, we can only truly love the other by being vulnerable to the other person, as Christ was with us on the Cross. By surrendering ourselves completely and humbly, as symbolized by the downward gaze, we enter into the vow of chastity understood as a gift beyond the sacrifice of romantic love and genital experiences, but as a total self-giving of ourselves to God, and, thus, to his people.

The vow of chastity thus invites us to move beyond ourselves, to learn to offer back to God what has been given to us so that we might be open to the movement of his Spirit and the needs of the many.

## OBEDIENCE

Obedience comes from the Latin words 'ob' and 'audire', which mean 'to listen to'. There is always room for discussion in our vows, but sometimes we are asked to do something we don't want to do, and we don't want to listen – which is a struggle. The smoke in this painting represents the Church, or our superiors, asking us to do something with what appears to be vague or incomprehensible motives, and we respond by just wanting to ask 'why?!' The subject in this image is huddled and closed off, resisting what he is hearing. Yet, his fingers are open – he is hearing what is being said. He is learning to be obedient not like a child, who constantly needs to be told what to do, but as an adult who is called to bind his will to those of others out of humble love; who respects the wisdom and will of the guardian, superior, and provincial as the guides leading their brothers on their vital and ever-moving journey to God.

# Bibliography

## Primary Sources

*The Works of St Bonaventure* (NY: Franciscan Institue Publications).

I, *On the Reduction of the Arts to Theology*, translation, introduction and commentary by Zachary Hayes OFM (1996).

VIII, parts 1–3, *Commentary on the Gospel of Luke*, ed. by Robert J. Karris OFM (2001, 2002, 2004).

IX, *Breviloquium*, ed. by Dominic V. Monti OFM (2005).

XIV, *Collations on the Seven Gifts of the Holy Spirit*, introduction and translation by Zachary Hayes OFM, notes by Robert J. Karris OFM(2008).

Cousins, Ewert, trans. and intro., *Bonaventure: The Soul's Joureny into God; The Tree of Life; The Life of St Francis* (NY: Paulist Press, 1978).

*St Francis of Assisi: Writings and Early Biographies. English Omnibus of the Sources for the Life of St Francis*, trans. by R. Brown, B. Fahy, P. Hermann, P. Oligny, N. de Robeck, L. Sherley-Price. Ed. by Marion A. Habig (Chicago: Franciscan Herald Press, 1983).

## Secondary Literature

Allen-Paisant, Jason, *Self-Portrait As Othello* (Carcanet Press, 2023).

Bloy, Léon, *The Woman Who Was Poor* (NY: Sheed & Ward, 1939).

Borghesi, Massimo, *Catholic Discordance* (MN, Collegeville: Liturgical Press, 2021).

Boyle, Gregory, *The Whole Language* (NY: Avid Reader Press, 2021).

Jackson, Drew, *God Speaks through Wombs* (Il, Downers Grove: InterVarsity Press, 2021).

McCarthy, Cormac, *The Road* (NY: Alfred A. Knopf, 2006).
— *The Passenger* (NY: Alfred A. Knopf, 2022).
— *Stella Maris* (NY: Alfred. A. Knopf, 2022).

Nouwen, Henri J. M., *The Wounded Healer* (London: DLT, 1994).

Oliver, Mary, *Devotions* (New York: Penguin Press, 2017).

Robinson, Marilynne, *Gilead* (London: Virago Press, 2006).